Visited by STAR TRAVELERS

DUANE ARTHUR OSE

STRATTON
—PRESS—
Publishing Life

Visited by Star Travelers
Copyright © 2019 **Duane Arthur Ose**

Stratton Press Publishing
831 N Tatnall Street Suite M #188,
Wilmington, DE 19801
www.stratton-press.com
1-888-323-7009

ISBN (Paperback): 978-1-64345-670-6
ISBN (Ebook): 978-1-64345-834-2

Printed in the United States of America

CHAPTER
1

As a boy born and raised in Minnesota, my future was set to continue helping my parents on the farm. I had no intention or other interests to do anything else but to be a farmer.

My hobbies were fishing, hunting, trapping, and art. I enjoyed and had a real talent for art. At one point a talent scout came out to our farm to persuade me to go to an art school. My interests were landscapes and painting beautiful women for calendars—some of which my friends paid good money for; hence, the talent scout discovered me. But after much debate, I passed on the offer, thus disappointing the agent.

As I became an adult, I worked for room and board, plus Dad let me use the farm equipment to do some custom work for the local farmers in the way of baling hay and straw. I was charging a dollar a bale. In turn, I bought the twine and paid another young neighbor friend of mine twenty-five cents per bale for bale handling. Dad would gift me the fuel for the tractor. My trapping made me money too; not much, but it was cash.

My last year on the farm was 1963. That was the year I was acting on a special request by a state game warden to become a beaver state nuisance trapper. That year I trapped 210 beavers and sold the meat to mink ranchers and shipped the excellent dried fur pelts to the fur auction house. Not much money, but I had no expenses.

Dad bought me a car, a '55 Chevy. He also supplied me the gasoline for being his right-hand man. I would earn extra cash for working for many farm neighbors' needs. It would sound like this: "Clarence, can you let me hire Duane for a bit?" I was happy to have the extra cash and willing to help.

My work ethic and diligence made my dad proud and paved my own way. I gained a lot of positive public relations by word-of-mouth endorsements and a lot of experience too. They kept me focused and strong from a good assortment of work projects and, most of all, occupied.

CHAPTER

2

It was the time of the military draft, and I was of age. Vietnam was cooking to blow up, and I did not want to be drafted to be in the infantry, so I opted to enlist to pick a noncombatant position. It would mean three years before I could help Dad farm again, but by enlisting, I'd be schooled in something I could use after I got out.

Dad and I talked a lot about that. He did not want me to enlist but wanted me to stay on the farm. I knew the odds of not being drafted was nil to none.

Dad farming alone was hard work, and he really needed me to stay.

For now, while I was still on the farm, Dad would give me time off for hunting deer with a bow. It was in season during the early mornings and some evenings.

This one morning, a day I shall never forget... It was a clear, bright, starlit October morning at 4:00 a.m. The year was 1963. I was only three months away from my twenty-first birthday when I turned the key on my '55 Chevy and quietly drove away as not to wake Mom and Dad on the Ose farm.

It was a crisp October morning in archery deer-hunting season. I had six miles to drive before I could park the car. Then there was a mile to walk in the dark using only the stars to light my way.

To legally kill a deer was hours away. But my goal was to be in place and ready before the deer came from their feeding areas to the woods to sleep for the day.

I exited the farm by driving out the dirt field road east to a Yellow Medicine County gravel road. Then I drove north past a working gravel pit that was created by the ancient River Warren and past the small, old, empty Anderson house. I drove on to where the bottom Minnesota River Valley East-West quarry road began. Going east again, I drove through some row cropland and crossed over a creek bridge. The creek flowed north past the Kollin farm site, a place I dreamed of buying someday and make it my home after I became rich. The big red barn, the beautiful house, and the bridges of granite stone were made by my grandfather Knute A. Ose. Knute Ose was born in Norway and became the local area stonemason. Besides being a landowner-farmer, his legacy in the form of stoneworks is still standing.

The Quarry Road was mostly surrounded by cedars and granite bedrock for two miles. Then I turned north on the Belview Sacred Heart Highway a half mile and drove over the Minnesota River Bridge. Then on one more mile, I made my final turn to the west on a Renville County gravel road that followed the bottom of the high south face of the Minnesota River Valley bluff, which was the ancient River Warren, north bank of River Warren of a million years ago.

Everything was going fine. It was very quiet. There were no other cars out at this hour or farmers in the fields. After shortly crossing over a huge concrete culvert for livestock with a now-flowing shallow creek running through it was a farmhouse lower than the road. Next, to the road, its bedroom windows were level to the grade of the road facing my driver's side of the car. The house was dark, so I knew that no one was up.

In the quiet still of the morning, I drove slowly and carefully on the smooth gravel-packed tire tracks so as to not awaken the two who lived there.

Then out of the blue, my Chevy stalled right by the bedroom windows. With no warning, it just stopped; even the headlights went off!

Nothing electrical worked on my car. I had no lights and no working starter. *Now what?* I thought. Quietly I exited the car and opened the hood. The hood made a creaking noise. I glanced at the house. Still no lights were on. Then I checked my battery posts for a solid connection. Nothing was wrong that I could determine. Then I closed the hood and went to try the starter again—nothing. Nada, not a sound and the car's lights still were not working.

The only lights I had were the twinkling stars.

Getting frustrated, and near sleeping people, I again opened the hood and this time jiggled all the wiring, including the spark plug wires, battery cables, coil wire, and all the connections. I then closed the car hood quietly. *Click*.

When I opened the car door, the dome light automatically came on, as it should day or night when the door is opened. That dome light was not even on before. When I turned the key and with no hesitation, the motor started, without a problem. I quietly drove off, not making a sound, and at some distance sped off to my parking spot only one and a quarter miles ahead.

Eventually, I concluded that it was a loose battery cable connection, but I was very puzzled as I found no loose or corroded connections. Before this day would end, however, I came up with a possible reason for losing all the car's electrical power.

Time was no longer on my side. I still had to park the car, follow my long, narrow, well-used dirt path up a steep bluff to the top. Then I had to cross a barbed wire pasture fence and walk another half a mile more.

Upon arriving and entering a large clearing, I walked down into a valley to an on-the-ground deer stand to the west all before about 4:30 a.m., or in my delayed case this morning, about 5:00 a.m.

After parking, I removed my hunting bow and arrows. I instantly felt I was not alone and was feeling uneasy about that. No biggie, I was finally here and still had to walk about another three quarter of a mile more. Alongside the car, I unzipped and watered the ground; I did not wish to have Mother Nature interrupt me on my walk.

During my walk up the bluff, I continued feeling uneasy. The further I walked, the more uneasy I felt. I crossed over that barbed wire fence, being careful not to rip any clothing.

Now on top of the bluff, I was in a pasture of short grass with a mix of oak, basswood, elm, cottonwood, maple, and cedar trees. Setback and just short of the top of the steep bluffs was a large electric service transmission line that ran east and west from a power plant to the twin cities following the Minnesota River Bluffs.

Also, this area, and others like it, was made up of parcels of wooded lots used for firewood and lumber of which my parents owned six acres of what we called the Ose "Woodlot." My Ose grandparents first owned the parcel. Now my parents have passed it on; it is now owned by us Ose kids.

Walking on now, with darkness all around, I only had the stars and a narrow opening of a tree-harvested pasture grass lane to guide me. The dark had never bothered me. The darkness had provided me protection many times. But the further I walked, the feeling of being watched became stronger. My thinking was a deer was watching me. I have had deer watch me before. Instead of letting the deer know that I know, I let them follow me. In preparation, I knocked an arrow in my laminated, fully recurved, 57-pound at full draw bow and ducked behind a tree and waited for the deer to walk past, shooting it if it was a worthy one of a good size.

This time I continued to walk to my destination. The feeling was so intense that I wanted to say aloud, "Hello! Show yourself." I knew it was not a deer watching or following me. Never have I had such a strong, intense feeling like that.

It was now after 4:30 a.m., and I was about to enter the clearing when I saw green grass clearing with fallen brown oak leaves. I could see color. Color! I then realized that a light was on me. My first thought, *Game warden!* But where was he? I looked for shadows to see where the light was originating. There were no shadows at all. I was standing on the edge of a soft but bright white light like it was midday.

It was then that I raised my eyes under my Australian Safari hat, and then my head and looked up. At the same time, I looked behind me to see a wall of darkness. I was standing in a 300-foot circle. It was dark outside the circle of light and light at the same time. The light was a strange pure white light not lighting up beyond the 300-foot round diameter. The light was like a liquid type of air light. Within that lit area, save for the 150-foot center where it was dark, there were no shadows under anything within the lighted area. In that 300-foot-across ring of light, there was a 50-foot-wide ring of light a few feet inside of the white light. Behind me, it was dark, very dark, which was where I was standing.

Wherever there was air within that light, there was light. A light of this type I have never experienced until now. A light that did not emit or shine beyond the lit area. The light and dark did not mix.

Then high over the trees, a huge round object that looked like a flying round craft was hovering silently in place. The craft itself was about 150 feet wide, 65 feet from top to bottom. The light was emitting from the mid outermost rim around the craft where the top and bottom joined. The light pointed at a 30-degree angle outward, and down to the ground engulfing a 300-foot round ring area about 50 feet wide.

The whole rim of the hovering craft was one light; no individual lighting was spaced around. It originated from one extended narrow rim of about twelve inches extending from the outermost surface of the round craft. There was no light from the bottom side like one might expect. The underside to the ground remained dark. I suspect it had sensors to detect any protruding hazards or surface materials.

As time passed, and as it came closer, I heard a deep, powerful, continuous hum during the descent of the craft. It had no wings, fins, windows, intake ports, exhaust ports, seams, heat shield, or rivets. The craft was shaped like two metal bowls. The rim of one bowl is to the inverted rim of the other bowl and was all in one piece—flat top and bottom like stainless steel mixing bowls.

It hovered above the treetops and slowly descended into a large treeless clearing. It had no wheels, pods, or landing gear. It "landed" but was hovering at the same time.

I just stood there inside the edge of the light, watching in amazement like a deer frozen in the headlights.

A few feet behind me was the darkness of only the starry sky.

The humming sound was like a gyro wheel or a spinning top. The sound changed as it set down. It changed from humming to idling but never completely silent. When it was hovering above the trees, it was louder. Whatever was making the hum, it was working hard during the hovering and lowering to the ground.

The sound was comparable to an airplane or chopper shutting off its engine; this hum never fully stopped, even while on the ground. I saw no spinning or wobbling as it came to the ground. The hum was within the wall of the craft. Not inside but within its round wall.

Now for the interesting part.

CHAPTER
3

It should be noted, I no longer had that uneasy feeling of being watched, and instead, it was as though I was looking at the new cars on a showroom floor. Due to my natural curiosity and my interest in engineering, I wanted to know all about this craft. How it worked, who made it, where it came from, and I wanted to meet the owner—or in this case, the pilots and crew.

To my right front, a door slowly opened near the bottom of the lower "bowl" without a sound or escaping gasses. The door was a tiltable one-piece door that was a gradually sloping ramp with no handrails, no cables, and wide enough for a sport all-terrain vehicle (ATV). The door opening was six feet high or more for headroom for a pilot. The ship had no windows. It was unlike any flying aircraft I've ever seen.

Then to my amazement, a short yellow two-legged life-form (or I had first thought) came down the ramp and walked toward me. There was about twenty-five feet between us.

Remember, I was armed with a powerful, 57-pound strength at full draw, hunting bow with six mounted bow quiver arrows and a razor-sharp hunting knife on my belt.

Here is my description of what approached me:

It, he, or *she* was four feet tall, slender, more like skinny. No hair, no skin pores, no clothes, no gender, and pale yellow skin (if skin). Limber arms and legs. Oval, long, enlarged head, hardly a forehead for its size, and the front part of the "eyes" were dark. Back from the dark part of the eyes was the clear to the white part of the eyes. I have seen a lot of eyes before, but none like these.

The slender, elongated head sloped back, no ears. No bathroom waste discharge holes, in front or behind. A slightly raised but flat nose with two up and down, side by side, short narrow slits for the nostrils. The mouth was a small inch-round open hole, no lips. The chin was pointed, long and narrow, no jawbone, slender neck, and rounded shoulders.

Legs had no muscle, nor did the arms. It had right and left flat feet that were small. No toes, but slender shaped feet with ankles above the round heels. I reiterate, the feet were shaped like right and left feet but no separation of toes or webs nor toenails. Almost like a skintight bodysuit, but it was not. The bone structure looked to be an unbreakable durable rubber, no mass. It seemed to have been made to be a robot, not a being that was born.

Here is the no clothes part of the description: There was no body hair, no gender/genitals, no breasts (male or female), no flab or excess skin, no belly bulge, and no rib cage showing. I detected no teeth. The mouth was not large enough for it to have teeth.

When I say it was made of durable rubber, it appeared to be a smart robot with an organized recon of data capabilities of highly advanced intelligence.

The elongated upward oval eyes had large black round pupils with white around the pupils in front. The bigger part to the rear of the eyes appeared to be of a clear void with bulblike electronic transmitter recording devices, showing long narrow gage wiring or veins (much like the elements in a light bulb). I felt like I was in front of a video camera being recorded remotely—no longer one on one.

This intelligent artificial robot was recording, sending, and receiving all the time. Its two eyes gave it balance capabilities and the ability to judge distance, to focus like we would with two eyes for depth perception. (With me having just one functional eye, I know there is no depth perception, only by reference, and lots of experience.) All creatures on earth have two eyes, but for the octopi, which have one eye.

All the while, this intelligent robot approached me and was saying to me, "Do not fear," repeatedly, in perfect American English and no accent. Not verbally but telepathically, from its mind to my mind.

When it got close, I sized it up and thought to myself, *I can take him.* It, he, or she heard me think that and quickly took one step back and this time loudly to my mind said, "Fear not!" with an expression on its face, for the first time, of shock.

I will now refer to "it" as a male, as the voice in my head sounded like a young man. Then cautiously, he came to me, extending his hand for me to hold. It was at that time I noticed he had small, slender hands of only three longer-than-normal, jointed fingers, no thumbs. The fingertips had no fingernails, but round, ball fingertip ends.

When our hands touched, clasping hands, I felt his finger ball tips had raised dots on the undersides for gripping or used as sensors. His palms were half the size of mine in comparison, allowing for the total size of the hand's difference. Only having three fingers, I could understand why.

His hand and fingers felt wimpy. They were weak and delicate.

I then realized I was about to be led into the craft. I rested my hat and the bow and arrows beside an oak tree, forgetting to remove the encased hunting knife that was on my belt. That knife was like a part of me; therefore, it was natural to forget to remove it. I do not know why I left the bow and arrows by the tree. I was not told to do so; it was just a habit of mine before entering any house.

He held my right hand in his left hand and again assured me, "No fear." It was like a youngster leading me to the door ramp, looking at me saying in a soothing tone in my head, "No fear."

This little guy led me inside and handed me over to six five-and-a-half-foot-tall robots like him, but these were green. When I say robots, that was what they seemed to be. But each had their personality. Again, no gender. All six green robots were of the same height and size.

CHAPTER

4

On my way inside the craft, I saw a spotlessly clean floor, no chairs or control panel stations, no cameras, no monitor screens, lamps, or light fixtures. Once in the craft, I had no problem adjusting to the light as it was all the same. I was absorbing everything, and my ears were still hearing a low gyro-like hum, almost silent, just barely noticeable. I sensed it was one or more ball objects racing around and around inside the outer wall (power source?). In time I paid no attention to the hum. No beings were talking to me, but I could tell that they were communicating with each other telepathically.

The green team of six guided me to a bench tabletop, a metal like an exam table that was waist-high to me. One was telepathically saying to me, "No fear."

While on the table, there was an all-encompassing light with no shadows or darkness anywhere. The light was not blinding or brighter in any one place. I know I wrote this before, but the light was like it was the air; it was a total all-engulfing light with no apparent source.

One of the greens pointed to the bench top, saying, "No fear." I walked to the side of the exam table and lifted myself sitting on it and swung my body lengthwise on it, fully dressed even in my boots on and my sharp hunting knife. I was not tied nor did I have any apprehension. I drank nothing nor was injected or gassed.

Lying on my back looking up, the green team surrounded me, three on each side. One of them looked above so I looked up to see why the green was looking up.

The level above us was a round, open gallery with a smooth round railing where there were taller beings (I'll call them the blue team, a group of blue beings). They were leaning over the handrail observing. The green team was getting instructions or advice from them also telepathically.

The only distinction between the light yellows, greens, and blues were their heights. Starting at four feet, then five and over six feet. There were no rank insignia or attire differences, only the color and size. All seemed to be artificial intelligence gathering, receiving, and sending robots. Sending to where I do not know, perhaps to their home base or into data storage.

As far as I know, there were no biological beings on the craft. I assumed these were deep space robots sending all information back to the planet whence they came.

Two of the greens on my right stood back while one held a wand-like device. It had no wiring or lighting. To me, it was a narrow rectangle of black wood: it was three feet long, two inches wide, and three-fourth inches in thickness.

At that time, I was told, "No fear." The one green held it at a level of three inches over me. The green brought it up past my head (I had no head support), looked up to the blues, paused, and then looked at his wand. Then he slowly moved it over me down past my feet. That was done twice more, maintaining a levelness of about three inches above me.

The green waited a bit then looked up to the blues. Some blues had walked out of my sight. We waited. I take it the blues were studying pictures or results of the scan.

With my eyes wide open, for there were no harsh bright lights, I looked for more details. I was not in a tightly closed room but, instead, off to one side in an open room with a high ceiling, save for just over me while lying on the exam table. I was on the bottom floor of no clutter but instead, fixed in place, enclosed secured items with no labeling. This craft was for fast, quick maneuvering. The only movable things were the occupants.

Things I did not see were doorknobs, handles, paneling, light fixtures, chairs, tables, benches, painted walls, just the fixed in place bench that I was on. Everything was metallic gray, with no padding. There were no vehicles or other means of transport. No bathrooms. No eating areas or bedrooms.

There were closed drawers like compartments but no knobs or handles. No compartments were ever opened within in my view.

This craft was for deep space exploration and instant travel. The whole ship was remotely controlled up to a point where the robots were the extended fingers of who-ever pushed the buttons from wherever.

I never went to the upper floors. I wish I had.

I have a question for you the reader. Why the one-inch mouth? They didn't drink liquids, eat food, discharge waste, or speak. Could the mouth be a charging port? Or made to resemble their builders?

My thoughts are, the humming was the power source to keep on the lights. The power used in an atmosphere with gravity, space travel, to include time travel by the tun-ing of the frequency of the hum. Toss in communications of both short ranges and to distant galaxies or universes. Plus, navigation. This craft traveled time, beyond the speed of light, motionless, and anywhere in between.

Somehow, for whatever reason, I have to believe I was picked out for study from before they stalled my car to now. The sense I had of being watched was them. They must have seen me as a suitable specimen for whatever data they were collecting. I hope I left them with a good impres-sion and understanding. Peace to them on whatever planet, galaxy, or universe they are based. But wait, this doesn't end here; there is more.

CHAPTER
5

The green team, after they were satisfied in what they were looking for, made a friendly gesture nodding their heads and escorted me to the open door of the ship. I nodded back. The same little yellow guy, whom I first met, took my hand and now hand-in-hand walked me back to my bow and arrows.

The short yellow guy then walked back to the ship's door, turned, paused, and looked back at me. For the first time, I spoke aloud and said as I waved with my right hand high over my head, "Goodbye and pleased to have made your acquaintance." He waved back nodding his head and went inside. As the door was closing, the humming began to increase in stages. The door fully closed; there was no sign that a door had ever been there.

The ground area still was lit. The hum became a whirring sound like a toy top spinning. Then back to a loud, steady hum. The craft began to leave the ground and ever so slowly rose up above the trees.

The ship hovered for five minutes with the lights on. My guess was running a systems check and charting its next destination, plus warming up. There was no breeze like when a plane or chopper takes off, only the sound.

The extended 300-foot ring of light went *tink!* Out with the outer rim light, yet on. The ship moved at a walking pace to the northeast for less than a hundred feet. Then in an instant, it disappeared.

It was now that I noticed it was early morning daylight and no stars.

CHAPTER
6

Even though I would be late getting to my stand that was about three hundred yards down in the forested valley, I went on. I stepped into my ground deer blind that overlooked a watering hole, sat down on my tree stump, gazed up, and saw the sun peeking over the treetops.

Perplexed about the time from 4:30 a.m. to now, I realized it was nearly 9:30 or 10:30 a.m. I remained there until high noon and went back to the farm to help Dad after we had dinner.

Dad was a supportive and understanding man, so I had no problem in talking to him about what happened on the woodlot.

Coincidentally, Dad, months before, had ordered a uranium Geiger counter as he or we were interested in finding uranium for making money. In the 1960s, it was the thing to do.

The next day, Dad and I decided to go to the wood-lot and check for radiation at the ship's landing site. But first, Dad checked my car's battery with a load tester and inspected the cable connections. The battery was strong, and there were no faulty connections. I drove. Along the way, we discussed my encounter over and over. Dad was absorbed and, at the same time, sort of testing me, I guess.

At the landing site, I walked him through everything again, showing him where the craft set down. He turned the Geiger counter on and poked the ground all over, detecting no radiation. We agreed no one would believe me, so I never told anyone else publicly but for my close friends.

Dad, of course, told Mom. Mom, when she and I were alone, asked me two questions:

Are you okay? Yes, I am fine.
Did they do anything to you? No, Mom.

Moms are like that.

CHAPTER

7

The next year, January 1964, I enlisted in the army. Trained and was assigned to work on air-defense missile bases in South Korea and near Wheeler, Indiana.

You guessed it. While on the base three miles north of Wheeler, after an incident, I and the few others involved were sworn never to divulge to our deaths what we witnessed. The initial orders were, "Erase the tapes and do not alert the civil populace." I can say no more. If I did, I am sure two plainclothesmen would have a talk with me.

Hint: Our radar tracked a craft of an unknown origin the length of Lake Michigan above the water and zipped up and past the city of Chicago in 1967, past Nike-Herc missile air defense site. I was the section chief of both the missile launch site and the radar section. Separated by two miles of cornfields, there was no time to raise a Nike-Herc missile out of the hardened, below ground launch site. It would have been futile anyway.

IN SUMMARY

We earthlings are not the only intelligent beings in all the universes around us. Humans here on earth may be far ahead of life on other worlds, but are far behind on the intelligence of the *star travelers*.